Table of Contents

GW00597243

4   Foreword by Lord Mayor of Dublin Caroline Conroy

6   About the Authors

9   **And Life Went On ... Daily life for Dubliners 1922**
CATHERINE SCUFFIL, Historian in Residence,
Dublin South City Areas

22   **'Eight young men in the City Hall ... with wild men
screaming through the keyhole' – Dublin City Hall in 1922**
CORMAC MOORE, Historian in Residence, Dublin North Central

36   **Women activists in Dublin during the Civil War**
MARY MULDOWNEY, Historian in Residence, Dublin Central area

50   **Remembering Cathal Brugha**
JAMES CURRY, Historian in Residence, Dublin Northwest

64   **'It's part of who we are today'. Children making sense of
the Civil War**
DERVILIA ROCHE, Historian in Residence for Children

Réamhra / Foreword

In the past year we saw the centenary of the Irish Civil War, the traumatic conflict which began in 1922 and continued to haunt Dublin and the rest of the country for many years.

This fifth volume in the *History on your Doorstep* series reflects the extensive research conducted by the four Historians in Residence and the Historian in Residence for Children into the events of the Civil War. The five chapters cover diverse approaches to the history of the tragedy as it affected Dublin between the commencement of the Civil War on 28 June 1922 to the call for an 'arms dump' in May 1923 that ended the hostilities, although there was no formal surrender.

Cormac Moore outlines the role played in 1922 by Dublin City Hall as the headquarters of the newly formed Provisional Government and as a symbol of the new statehood the pro-Treaty side was trying to establish.

Catherine Scuffil looks at the everyday experiences of the citizens of Dublin in the course of the Civil War as ordinary life continued against a backdrop of civil unrest and violence. Despite the dangers, the new state succeeded in laying the foundations of welcome social initiatives, such as the building of much needed estates of new homes.

Women activists played various roles during the years from 1913 to 1923 but the Civil War saw them becoming more involved in military duties. Mary Muldowney discusses their involvement, including drawing from some of the women's own accounts in their applications for Military Service Pensions.

James Curry remembers the life and career of anti-Treaty Cathal Brugha, and his death in July 1922 as the first high profile casualty of the Civil War. His body lay in state in the Mater Hospital where he died, accompanied by an honour guard of Cumann na mBan members, at the request of his wife, herself a member of the organisation. Brugha is commemorated at various sites around Dublin.

The chapter by the Historian in Residence for Children, Dervilia Roche covers her experience of explaining war to young children and helping them to understand the issues that drove the Irish Civil War. Dervilia ran a series of workshops focussing on the 'Battle of Dublin' in 1922, using both the involvement of local places in Dublin, as well as the significant anniversary of the battle, as a means for the children to connect with the topic.

This fifth volume of *History on Your Doorstep* will be available free from all Dublin City Libraries and as an e-book from the Library's website at http://dublincity.spydus.ie

CAROLINE CONROY
Lord Mayor of Dublin

History on your Doorstep, Volume 5 is produced by Dublin City Libraries and is published by Dublin City Council as part of its Decade of Commemorations programme with the support of the Department of Tourism, Culture, Arts, Gaeltacht, Sport and Media.

This volume was project managed by Linda Devlin and Darragh Doyle, Dublin City Council Culture Company.

About the authors

JAMES CURRY received his PhD in History & Digital Humanities from NUI Galway in 2017, having previously graduated with BA and MPhil history degrees from Trinity College Dublin. He is the creator of a "History of Dublin" channel on YouTube and has published widely on twentieth century Irish history, including a book about Dublin radical cartoonist Ernest Kavanagh. James is a former committee member of the Irish Labour History Society and is the Historian in Residence for the North West area of Dublin City.

CORMAC MOORE has a PhD in History from De Montfort University in Leicester and an MA in Modern Irish History from UCD. He is Historian in Residence for Dublin North Central and is author of *Birth of the Border: The Impact of Partition in Ireland*, *The Irish Soccer Split*, and *The GAA V Douglas Hyde: The Removal of Ireland's First President as GAA Patron*.

MARY MULDOWNEY holds a PhD in History from Trinity College Dublin and a postgraduate qualification in Adult Continuing Education and Training from the National University of Ireland at Maynooth. She is the Historian in Residence for the Dublin Central area. Mary is the author of books and journal articles and she has a particular interest in labour and women's history. She is a member of the Grangegorman Histories Expert Working Group, the committee of the Irish Labour History Society (ILHS) and she is co-editor of *Saothar*, the journal of the ILHS. She was a founding member of the Oral History Network of Ireland and is a frequent consultant on other history projects.

DERVILIA ROCHE has been working in heritage and public history for over fifteen years. She has a BA in History of Art and Architecture and Music from Trinity College Dublin, and an MSc in Tourism Management from Dublin Institute of Technology. She has undertaken and published research on how children engage with heritage sites, and has worked across the city in education roles at historic sites and museums. She was appointed as Dublin's first Historian in Residence for Children, as part of Dublin City Council Culture Company's Creative Residency programme, in partnership with Dublin City Libraries and Richmond Barracks.

CATHERINE SCUFFIL. Dublin born and reared, Catherine's interest in local history was formed at an early age encouraged by parents who also shared a love of Dublin. She was honorary secretary/founder member of the Dolphin's Barn Historical Society (1986) compiling and editing their publication By the Sign of the Dolphin (1993) In addition to an honours Business and Management degree, Catherine also holds both a Certificate and a Masters in Local History from NUI Maynooth. Her master's thesis research was published by Four Courts Press as *The South Circular Road Dublin on the Eve of the First World War* and an abridged version was awarded the silver medal by the Old Dublin Society (2018). Catherine was actively involved in a wide range of community events during the 1916 Rising centenary commemorations, researching the Rialto/Kilmainham 1916 Commemoration photographic exhibition and a publication *1916 in the South Dublin Union* for St. James's Hospital. Catherine is currently working as Historian in Residence with Dublin City Council for the South Central and South East Areas and is a consultant historian for other projects.

The Historian in Residence programme is part of Dublin City Council's work under the Decade of Commemorations (1912-22) designation and strives to break down barriers to history. The programme was created by Dublin City Libraries and is delivered in partnership with Dublin City Council Culture Company.

Contact the Historians in Residence at
historians@dublincitycouncilculturecompany.ie
Follow on Facebook and Twitter at @dubhistorians

Dublin City Council Historians in Residence Cormac Moore, Mary Muldowney, Cathy Scuffil and James Curry with Historian in Residence for Children Dervilia Roche at the launch of *'History on your Doorstep: Volume 4'*. Image by Marc O'Sullivan

Tara Byrne and Erin Crotty with the Historian in Residence for Children, Dervilia Roche. Image by Marc O'Sullivan

And Life Went On ...
Daily life for Dubliners 1922

Catherine Scuffil, Historian in Residence, Dublin South City Areas

Dublin, January 1922, was a city in anticipation.

Following almost three long difficult years of conflict during the War of Independence, and the subsequent Truce and Treaty negotiations, the possibilities that an independent Irish Free State would bring – when achieved - were keen topics of discussion amongst the city's anxious and concerned citizens.

16 January 1922, dawned as a bleak, frosty, cold morning in Dublin, but this did not stop crowds of people gathering around the gates of Dublin Castle. Tension filled the air. It seemed that something momentous was about to happen. Then, as white powdery flakes dropped from the sky and landed on the crowd, it initially seemed that it was the beginning of a snow shower. Slowly, it transpired that this was not indeed snow, but flakes of ash falling from the sky. This was the by-product from a line of burning bonfires in the castle yard. The British authorities, the – for now - current occupants of Dublin Castle were clearing out files and papers, and what they could not carry or bring with them was burned in the pyres that had been set around the castle. The city's newspapers reported that what once seemed impossible, was in fact, actually about to happen. Dublin Castle was, finally, handed over to the care of the Irish people.

As the news slowly filtered out to the crowds outside, at the lower castle yard gates near Dublin's City Hall thousands of Dubliners cheered joyfully. The castle – a symbol and the seat of British rule in Ireland for so many centuries - now saw the withdrawal of the military guard at the various entrances for the first time since the beginning of the War of Independence. The barbed wire which entangled the gates had not yet been removed from the entrance to the upper gate, where many sandbags were still *in situ*. Suddenly, Dubliners saw a military party engaged in the work of removing these items when the members of the Provisional Government drove in to take over the reins of Government. The newspapers reported that the official function in the Privy Council Chamber was brief and 'devoid of all ceremonial' as Mr. Michael Collins formally received the power of Government and took over the various Departments which were part of the Castle system. The new Provisional Government, would, in the weeks that followed, have all the administrative departments under its direct control. Ireland was on the path to nationhood. Dublin was, once again, an independent capital city.

The days and months that followed saw a continuous line of ships and steamers along the quays of Dublin, with special trains arranged from country towns to take the departing members of the British garrison back home. One of the first to arrive was a train from Kildare carrying soldiers, officers, mules and horses, as well as a range of other items of military equipment. Two hundred and twenty men of the Duke of Wellington's regiment from the Curragh Military Camp were about to depart. The 47,000 strong British Military personnel located at various barracks around the country were 'clearing out, lock, stock and barrel' and would completely leave Ireland by the end of 1922.

In the days that followed, Dubliners soon noticed long detailed advertisements in the daily newspapers. These encouraged people to support the Irish economy. Headlines suggested that citizens make a belated new year resolution for 1922. Every purchase, no matter how small, should be planned and made with Irish manufacture in mind. Each item you thought you needed, and a few that perhaps you never would, were listed alongside the name, address and contact details of the Irish manufacturer or stockist. Citizens were encouraged to cut out the list and keep it at home, close at hand, for future reference.

On 31 January 1922 the city's newspapers carried reports of even more excitement on the streets of Dublin. A small contingent of the new National Army of Ireland – about 46 members – had assembled in the Phoenix Park on Chesterfield Avenue directly in front of the Wellington Monument. The group lined up in strict order behind a kilt band and prepared for an inaugural march down the Liffey quays towards the centre of the city. As the group passed the Royal Barracks on the north quays, the sound of the marching band attracted the attention of British soldiers still garrisoned there, awaiting their departure to barracks back home in Britain. Bored, with little else to do but wait, they were engaged in a game of football in the courtyard. They abandoned the game and ran over to the railings to watch the passing parade before it reached Grattan Bridge where huge crowds of cheering Dubliners awaited. The small army group then marched up Parliament Street to City Hall where members of the Provisional Government waited to take the salute following the sharp 'eyes right!' command. From here, the group marched on to Beggars Bush Barracks where the tricolour flag was proudly hoisted in what was, for now, the new headquarters of the Free State Army.

British era post boxes in Chapelizod, painted green in 1922 (Left: Victoria Regina and right: Edward Rex) courtesy of John Buckley

As the country prepared for the first St. Patrick's Day as a new Free State, another change happened on the streets. One-by-one the city's pillar-boxes were painted green replacing the former traditional red. St. Patrick's Day 1922 was a day of huge celebration both at home and abroad. Children wore ribbons displaying the national colours and large queues formed outside the city churches, of all denominations, where the sermon and hymns were presented in Irish. Newspapers carried accounts of greetings passing between Dublin and other places overseas, with Michael Collins thanking the people of the United States in particular for their support of Ireland. St. Patrick's Day 1922 was a day that marked a new beginning for a new state.

All was not well in Ireland at this time from a political viewpoint. The terms and implementation of the Treaty were still contentious issues for many and on 14 April 1922 anti-Treaty IRA militants, under Rory O'Connor, occupied the last remaining intact public building on Dublin's northside, the Four Courts. Reporters expressed concern that the Four Courts seemed destined to suffer a similar fate to other public buildings that bore the scars of the recent conflicts. The General Post Office in O'Connell Street had been reduced to a shell during the 1916 Rising, with little but the exterior walls left intact. The Custom House further downstream on the river Liffey near the docks had been largely destroyed by fire during the War of Independence.

The occupiers of the Four Courts were trying to unite two IRA factions, the IRA executive and those described as anti-Treaty, with the aim of restarting the fight against the former common enemy and ultimately achieve the goal of an all-Ireland Republic. They anticipated that a new armed confrontation with British forces would ultimately bring down the Anglo-Irish Treaty. Thousands of British Army personnel were still in Dublin awaiting their turn for evacuation. Ultimately there were now three 'armies' in Ireland, the remains of the British garrison, the new National Army and now the Four Courts Republicans. For now, however, this was just an occupation of the Four Courts. This would escalate several months later into a much more serious conflict that officially marked the beginning of the Irish Civil War.

In May 1922, there was a general invitation carried in the daily newspapers to a public meeting in the Church of Our Lady of Dolours, Dolphin's Barn. The meeting intended to discuss ways to raise funds to clear the debt of the then newly opened parochial boy's school on the South Circular Road, Rialto and all were welcome to attend.

The new school had been recently built on land donated by the local Alderman and Rialto resident, Michael Flanagan, and marked a new beginning to raise the standard of boys' education in the Irish Free State. The meeting was extremely well attended, with many key personalities of the time taking the opportunity to speak to the gathered crowd. Included

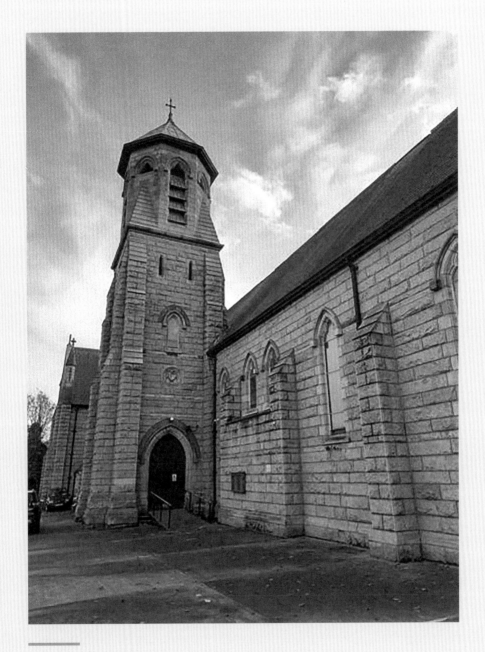

Dolphin's Barn Church courtesy of John Buckley

among them was William T. Cosgrave, who expressed his particular thanks to Dolphin's Barn residents and others in the locality who had given him shelter during the troubled times when it was not safe for him to return to his mother's home in James's Street. The collection and pledges that followed cleared the school debt in the first year of classes.

Following the assassination of Field Marshal Sir Henry Hughes Wilson in London on 22 June 1922 it quickly became apparent that Winston Churchill held the Anti-Treaty garrison within the Four Courts responsible for his death. In response, he warned Michael Collins that action must be taken against this group as soon as possible, or arrangements would be made for the remaining British garrison in Ireland to re-take control of Dublin and by default, Ireland. Tensions once again began to rise in Dublin, culminating on 26 June when the Four Courts garrison kidnapped Free State General JJ "Ginger" O'Connell. The following day, 27 June, Michael Collins issued a final ultimatum to the Four Courts garrison to surrender. This was generally ignored, and consequently, direct action was employed by the Free State forces, thus marking the beginning of the Irish Civil War. Three – with two ultimately being used – British 18-pounder field guns were acquired and a shelling bombardment commenced on the Four Courts building by the Free State National Army under the instructions of Paddy O'Daly.

The upheaval of the so-called 'Battle of Dublin' had a ripple effect across the country. Passenger trains timetables were suspended and other public buildings, such as post-offices in various locations nationwide were immediately seized by Anti-Treaty forces, or irregulars as they were called by Treatyites. Newspapers reported that the Drogheda railway bridge was destroyed, effectively cutting off the rail link with the north of the country.

As these events were playing out, at the then small hamlet called Red Cow on the Naas Road near Clondalkin village, twelve members of the Anti-Treaty F-Company 4th Battalion of the IRA commenced an attack on a Free State outpost located in a nearby farmhouse. This was to secure the approaches to the city on behalf of the Anti-Treaty forces. Among the group was a young man from a well-known and popular family in Inchicore, John Monks. He was employed as an apprentice blacksmith in the Railway Works in Inchicore, with Monks himself a resident in the locality. The area around the works and Inchicore generally was much associated with activities of the 4th Battalion IRA who had, in the main, opted not to support the Treaty.

It was very quickly discovered, shortly after the attack at Red Cow had commenced, that the irregulars were seriously outnumbered as, unknown to them, the outpost was fully manned with Free State forces. An intense battle broke out and in the crossfire that followed, John Monks was fatally injured by a gunshot wound to the neck. His body was found some time later in a small field on the Inchicore side of the road and retrieved by Ms. Flood from Portlester House further down the Naas Road at Bluebell, who had travelled to the site by horse and cart. She collected John Monks' body on behalf of the family. A few days later, John Monks was laid to rest in Bluebell cemetery in a grave newly purchased by his grieving father. John Monks was the first official casualty of the Irish Civil War.

Meanwhile, back in Dublin city centre, a wedding was taking place at St. Andrew's Church, St. Andrew's Street, and this too would be directly affected by the turmoil elsewhere in the city. It was reported that two motor cars, intended for the wedding party, were hi-jacked and taken from outside the church while the marriage ceremony was underway inside between Mr. Wilfred [Harry] Barnardo and Miss Peggy McDonald. Mr. Barnardo was well-known in Dublin society circles due to his close associations with more than half a dozen charitable institutions in the city, as well as the fact that he was one of the leading furriers in Ireland. Following the ceremony, Mr. Barnardo and his wife said to a *Daily Mail* reporter

> *"We were married under a big bombardment, guns were firing all the time, but we are quite happy. We are leaving for London to-night"*

As the bombardment of the Four Courts continued, sensational incidents were witnessed in Dolphin's Barn. The village was a strategic and prime location from the point of view of securing the city for the anti-Treaty forces. It was located on the outskirts of Dublin's Liberties, at an intersection of two key roads – the route from Crumlin which was a direct link to the aerodrome and military stores in Baldonnell and the South Circular Road with access to Richmond Barracks at Inchicore and Wellington Barracks near Leonard's Corner. It was also in the heartland of the F Coy 4th Battalion IRA. It appears that early in the day a party of irregular troops entered the premises of the Royal Bank - a newly erected building - and established themselves in it as a vantage post. Shortly afterwards a large force of Free State troops arrived and took up positions in front of the building. This group were supported by two armoured cars. They proceeded to open fire on the building with machine-guns and other weapons. After some time, the anti-Treaty forces made their escape via the back of the building, but before they did so the popular provision and post-office establishment of Messrs. Coleman on the opposite side of the road, caught fire. The large crowd of locals who had gathered in the area cheered as the Fire Brigade arrived to extinguish the flames.

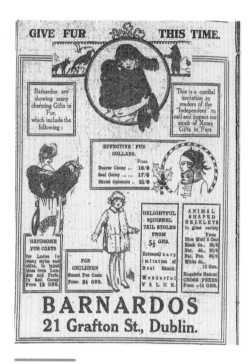

Barnardo's Advertisement, *Irish Independent*, Monday 18 December 1922 courtesy of Irish Newspaper Archive Online

The bank at Dolphin's Barn also featured in the news for another reason. The case of those arrested under suspicion of involvement in a hold up of the premises in 1921 was being widely reported on. Shortly after the new branch office of the Royal Bank had opened, it had been the subject of a hold-up by men armed with revolvers, with the manager and cashier forced to pass over the sum of £19 5s from the interior safe. The same day, a similar incident occurred at another bank branch in Camden Street, a short distance away. One suspect was already convicted and serving a term of imprisonment, two others were currently before the courts. Another was still at large. The case and investigations were ongoing.

The Battle of Dublin lasted just six days and by the middle of July, Dubliners eagerly sought information about the salvage operations that had started at the ruins of the Four Courts and badly damaged surrounding buildings. Among the items recovered were the heads of the judge's statues that had been damaged in the front rotunda. It was also reported that in the debris of the Public Records Office nearly 1000 bound copies of valuable documents were found. The bindings were severely scorched and portions were burned here and there, but, overall, these documents were, happily, intact, small 'survivors' in an otherwise huge loss to the ancient records of Ireland.

Free State Housing,
The Tenters
courtesy of John Buckley

In other news, it was noted that Dublin now faced a 'heavy bill' for damage caused during the shelling of the Four Courts and related incidents elsewhere in the city during the week. The rapidly increasing bill was now approaching a million pounds in claims. Among those lodged with the town clerk were claims from the Gresham Hotel in O'Connell Street and a considerable number from the Royal Bank of Ireland for damage caused to branch offices in Smithfield, O'Connell Street and the newly opened branch premises at Dolphin's Barn where damage amounting to £2,500 had occurred during the disturbances.

Amidst all the destruction and general upheaval around the city, there was some good news for Dubliners. Dublin Corporation had commenced construction of an estate of new homes in Fairbrother's Fields, also known as The Tenters, an area that during the First World War had been utilised as market-gardens and allotments. The site was located between Cork Street, Clanbrassil Street and the South Circular Road, Dolphin's Barn. The name 'Tenters' derived from the former industrial practice where weaver's cloth was hung out in the large open spaces on tenterhooks. This dated back to the time when the area was hugely linked to all aspects of the weaving industry.

The houses were being built in a carefully planned estate in response to the then extremely serious housing crisis in Dublin. Many residents were living in substandard accommodation with poor or, in some cases, no actual sanitation.

The Tenters is recognised for several 'firsts' in the provision of public housing. It was the first estate built in the new Free State and was the first 'tenant-purchase scheme' undertaken. People who had never anticipated owning their own home, now had the prospect of doing so. Also, for the very first time, planned cul-de-sacs were included in the estate layout, and this, together with the future promise of a new boy's school, a reserved site for a new Roman Catholic church, and the close proximity of both Dolphin's Barn and the Liberties with its shops, services and businesses, made the area a most attractive prospect for young couples and families with small children. The large development had the knock-on benefit of creating employment for builders and labourers. The locally sourced materials, such as Dolphin's Barn bricks resulted in a second kiln being reinstated in the brickworks with bonuses planned for workers at Christmas. Unfortunately, as the incidents of civil unrest continued, in December the brickworks offices were raided by anti-Treaty forces, who made off with the Christmas bonuses and wages due to the workforce.

During the summer of 1922, newspapers once again carried details of several prosecutions being taken against the dairy owners of Dolphin's Barn Hollow. The incident shared equal headline status with other serious

MORE POWER TO YOUR ELBOW, RECORDER!

DAIRY PROPRIETOR—"Oh, sir! It wasn't me, sir. It was me manager—the boy at the pump beyant. Shure Sir Charles said I did not personally connive."

THE RECORDER—"I don't want talk of that kind. You have been convicted before."

[The Recorder said this business of milk adulteration meant simply the absolute murder of young children. Not only was the defective milk a cause of wasting in children, but it was a direct producer of intestinal and other diseases most detrimental to infant life. As far as he was concerned, he would use every effort to stamp out this fraud evil in the city. . . . He had to look at the fact that dairy business in Dublin was not carried on by milk companies but appeared to be largely in the hands of unscrupulous people who hoped it a rapid way of getting rich at the expense of the poor.—Comments of the Recorder on a dairy-keeper's appeal against a conviction of his clerk for "milk adulteration."]

incidents of civic unrest, such as the destruction of rail lines and shootings, everyday events in the country as the Civil War continued. Not for the first time, the dairy owners were collectively fined for tampering with the fat content of their milk production by its removal and substitution with water. This practice was known as 'adulteration' and had been one of a range of ongoing issues of grave concern in the city since before the outbreak of the First World War. Milk was a daily staple and in times of shortages an important source of nutrition for all ages. Any interference with the quality and supply of milk was considered a serious offence at the time.

Despite the ongoing political and civil unrest directly related to the Civil War, the possibilities that an independent Irish Free State offered for the welfare of citizens were key talking points among the population. Life for Dubliners and others elsewhere around the country continued, and there was much concern as efforts were made to build a new nation with a stable economy. Education for Ireland's young people was high on the list of priorities as was the need for better quality housing and a higher standard of food production.

Daily life went on.

Further Reading

- DORNEY, JOHN, *The Civil War in Dublin*, The Academic Press, 2017
- GILLIS, LIZ, *The Fall of Dublin*, Mercier Press 2011
- O'DONNELL, PEADAR, *The Gates Flew Open*, Mercier Press, 2013
- O'MALLEY, ERNIE, *The Singing Flame*, Mercier Press, 1999
- SMITH, BRIAN, *Irish Civil War Executions, 1922-1923*, Self-Published 1922
- YEATES, PADRAIG, *A City in Civil War – Dublin 1921-1924; The Irish Civil War*, Gill and Macmillan

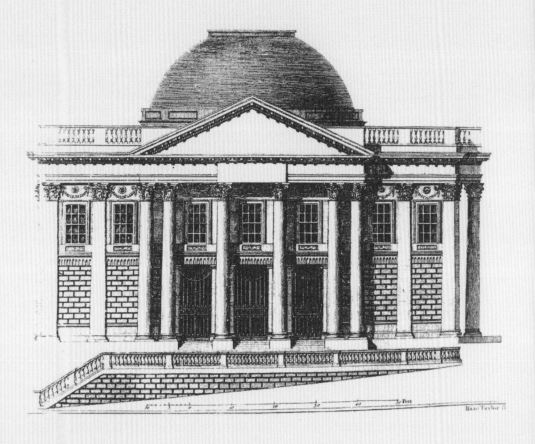

Dublin City Hall as the Royal Exchange around 1850
courtesy of Dublin City Library and Archives

'Eight young men in the City Hall ... with wild men screaming through the keyhole' – Dublin City Hall in 1922

Cormac Moore, Historian in Residence, Dublin North Central

In early 1922, Kevin O'Higgins described the Provisional Government of the Irish Free State, of which he was a member, as 'simply eight young men in the City Hall standing amidst the ruins of one administration, with the foundation of another not yet laid, and with wild men screaming through the keyhole'. This essay will look at the role Dublin City Hall played in 1922 as the headquarters of the newly formed Provisional Government. It was also a symbol of the new statehood the pro-Treaty side was attempting to embark upon in the face of a split that evolved into a civil war by the summer of 1922.

Dublin City Hall was built between 1769 and 1779. It was designed by a young London architect Thomas Cooley whose design was controversially chosen over that of James Gandon's. Originally built as the Royal Exchange, it was the main centre for trade in Dublin in the late 1700s. With the Act of Union, introduced in 1800, contributing to Dublin's economy plummeting, the building fell out of use until it was bought by Dublin Corporation in 1852, when it became the City Hall.

Before 1922, the building had been an important site for Irish nationalists. It was the site of the lying in state of the 'Uncrowned King of Ireland' Charles Stewart Parnell upon his death in October 1891, as it was upon the death of Jeremiah O'Donovan Ross in 1915 and of Thomas Ashe in 1917. Given its vantage point of being next door to Dublin Castle, where British troops would be entering and exiting, it was seized by members of the Irish Citizen Army under the leadership of Sean Connolly on the afternoon of Monday, 24 April 1916, as were other buildings in the immediate vicinity. Connolly shot dead Dublin Metropolitan Police (DMP) Constable James O'Brien, believed to be the first crown fatality of the Easter Rising, before Connolly himself became the first insurgent fatality in Dublin after he was shot while on the roof of City Hall.

During the anti-conscription crisis of 1918 in the First World War, on Lá na mBan, Women's Day, on 9 June 1918, around 8,000 women marched from Great Denmark Street near the Rotunda Hospital to Dublin City Hall to sign a pledge not to fill the job of any man made redundant for refusing to comply with conscription.

During the War of Independence, in an act of open defiance against British authority, the Irish tricolour was flown from the flagpole outside City Hall from February 1920. As the conflict escalated throughout the year, City Hall was occupied by British troops on 22 December 1920, the tricolour pulled down from the flagpole and barbed wire placed across all entrances. The citizens of Dublin became 'accustomed to the barbed wire entanglements which forbade an entrance to the area occupied by the City Hall buildings', according to the *Irish Times*. For just over a year, while held by the British, the rooms on the ground floor were used as quarters for soldiers and it became a site for courts-martial, including ones associated with Bloody Sunday, the Brunswick Street (now Pearse Street) ambush, and the trial of officers and men of the Auxiliaries for the shooting of a prisoner. Nine IRA members were sentenced to death in City Hall, including Sean McEoin.

With the ratification of the Anglo-Irish Treaty by Dáil Éireann on 7 January 1921 and the subsequent resignation of Éamon de Valera as Dáil president after losing a vote on his presidency, a new Dáil government was formed with Arthur Griffith as president. Days later, on 14 January, a meeting of the parliament of Southern Ireland consisting of pro-Treaty TDs and four unionist MPs from Trinity College Dublin met in the Mansion House. As

Poster for anti-Conscription Campaign Lá na mBan event
courtesy of National Library of Ireland

Barbed wire entanglements being removed from City Hall early in 1922 courtesy of Dublin City Library and Archives

the British government still refused to recognize the Dáil, this body, which never met again, ratified the Treaty and appointed a Provisional Government to which the British would hand over the powers and machinery needed for it to carry out its duties until the Free State formally came into being on 6 December 1922. As a concession to anti-Treatyites, Griffith abstained from membership of the provisional government but 'called on every good Irishman to put aside old differences and support the Provisional Government, predicting that its task would be very heavy'. Michael Collins was chosen as chairman of the provisional government.

Shortly afterwards, in a moment of symbolic significance, Dublin Castle was handed over to the provisional government on 16 January. On that date, a delegation led by Michael Collins met the Lord Lieutenant Lord FitzAlan in the Privy Council chamber in the upper yard of Dublin Castle for 55 minutes where the formal handover occurred.

Days later, on 21 January 1922, three years to the day since Dáil Éireann met for the first time and shots were fired at Soloheadbeag in Tipperary, Dublin City Hall was handed back to Dublin Corporation. At 10 am that morning, Lieutenant Colonel Bates, commander of British troops at Ship Street Barracks, handed over City Hall to W.T. Cosgrave in his capacity as Acting Lord Mayor of Dublin, due to Laurence O'Neill's attendance at the Irish Race Congress in Paris at the time. One of Cosgrave's first actions was to hoist the Dublin City flag on the roof of City Hall. A day later, Pope Benedict XV died and the flag over City Hall was flown at half-mast. On taking over City Hall, Cosgrave told the press that 'it would take a little while to get the place into proper order' again, given that there still was barbed wire around the building and the rooms needed to be cleaned and redecorated thoroughly. He also stated that Dublin Corporation 'will take possession in the first instance, and then the building will be placed at the disposal of seven Ministers, and the City Hall will become for the present the headquarters of the new [Provisional] Government'.

The *Evening Herald*, reporting on the day the Provisional Government took over City Hall, spoke of the movement and appearance of IRA sentries at Dublin City Hall attracting a crowd, with a noticeable stir evident when Collins arrived to take up his office. He took over the Town Clerk's office.

The *Evening Herald* also noted that 'while the City Hall is the Headquarters of the Provisional Government, Dáil Éireann and the government of the Dáil continue to function from the Mansion House'.

There were of course two pro-Treaty governments and cabinets at the time – The Dáil government with Griffith as president and the Provisional Government with Collins as chairman. The make-up of the Provisional Government cabinet was very similar in make-up to that of the Dáil cabinet. **Table 1** shows a list of Griffith's Dáil cabinet which remained based in the Mansion House, and a list of Collins's provisional government which took up temporary residence in City Hall. As can be seen from the table, there was a huge cross-over in personnel between the parallel pro-Treaty cabinets, with many holding identical portfolios in both. This was an attempt to bolster their legitimacy but ultimately it did not alleviate the confusing power structures at play in Ireland at the time.

Table 1

Position	Dáil Cabinet	Provisional Government Cabinet
President/ Chairperson	Arthur Griffith	Michael Collins
Finance	Michael Collins	Michael Collins
Foreign Affairs	George Gavan Duffy	
Home Affairs	Eamonn Duggan	Eamonn Duggan
Local Government	W.T. Cosgrave	W.T. Cosgrave
Economic Affairs	Kevin O'Higgins	Kevin O'Higgins
Defence	Richard Mulcahy	
Labour		Joseph McGrath
Agriculture		Patrick Hogan
Education		Finian Lynch
Postmaster General		J.J. Walsh

While not a member of the provisional government, Griffith still attended many of its meetings in City Hall. And even though Richard Mulcahy as Dáil Minister of Defence was not a member of the provisional government, he started to attend its meetings from mid-February 1922.

Speaking in the Dáil on 28 February, Griffith was confident that the departments in the parallel administrations were 'actively functioning in harmony' and, 'in the interests of peace and good order', would continue to do so until the general election. Many anti-Treaty TDs questioned the provisional government's authority, who was it answerable to, and refused to recognise it as a legitimate body. During Dáil exchanges, anti-Treaty TDs, such as Sean MacEntee, queried why Dáil Éireann staff were being transferred to City Hall, why Dáil cabinet ministers were responding to their correspondence as 'Ministers of the Provisional Government' addressed from City Hall, even though the Provisional Government directed people to continue to address all queries to it through the Mansion House. In a barbed letter to the *Irish Times*, Michael Collins responded to Cathal Brugha (who he called Mr. Charles Burgess) who rang the Mansion House to be told the Finance Department was not there, but in the City Hall. Collins wrote,

> *'I wish to say that the Finance Department of the Dáil was never at the Mansion House. All Dáil Departments, by the courtesy of the Lord Mayor of Dublin, were allowed to use the Mansion House as an official address. It is being used in this manner still. If Mr. Burgess has any business to do with the Department, he can either call to the Department itself or communicate in writing to the Mansion House'.*

Kathleen Clarke, who subsequently became the first female Lord Mayor of Dublin, at a Dublin Corporation meeting in late January 1922, raised the issue of City Hall being used by the provisional government as its headquarters. She made 'inquiries of the Town Clerk as to how this came about, and he said that the Estates and Finance Committee gave permission. She wished to know if the Committee had power to give that permission. She objected to its being given to the Provisional Government of the Free State. She objected when the British Government asked for it, and she made a similar objection now. The City Hall should not be in the hands of anyone but the Corporation'. She put forward a motion that 'the Provisional Government of the Free State be asked to remove themselves to where they had plenty of room – namely, the Castle, that had been handed over to them' but as she could find no seconder to her motion, it fell through, and no vote was taken.

From the moment the Provisional Government moved into City Hall on 23 January 1922, there was constant activity around the buildings as the nascent government looked to exert its newfound authority. A steady stream of visitors called to City Hall daily throughout the subsequent months. Consular staff from the United States, France, Persia and other countries visited, wishing the new state success and promising cooperation.

One of the most significant meetings held in City Hall was between Collins and the Northern Ireland Prime Minister James Craig on 2 February, just days after both signed the first Craig-Collins Pact in London. Huge crowds gathered to see the arrival of Craig, who met with Collins for almost three hours, but no agreement was reached on the Border. The violence in the North and the overall Border question dominated much of Collins's time as chairperson of the Provisional Government. Days later a deputation from Derry Corporation, led by its Lord Mayor Hugh O'Doherty, the first Catholic mayor of Derry since the seventeenth century, also visited Collins in City Hall, strongly objecting to Derry's inclusion in Northern Ireland. A member of Craig's cabinet in the North, the Minister for Agriculture Edward Archdale also visited his Free State counterpart, Patrick Hogan, in the City Hall in February 1922. As partition became more permanent and both jurisdictions moved further and further apart, Archdale and Hogan were the only two ministers who kept in regular contact with each other.

The British Army commander-in-chief in Ireland Nevil Macready visited Collins in City Hall too in early February to discuss the evacuation of British troops and the taking over of military depots by the IRA. In another symbolically important moment, IRA troops, en route from the Phoenix Park to take over Beggars' Bush barracks, passed by City Hall where they

Michael Collins addressing an election meeting 1922
courtesy of National Library of Ireland

were reviewed by Collins, Griffith and other ministers, as a large crowd looked on. As divisions escalated in the spring of 1922, the guard numbers were increased in March from the original twelve, which was deemed insufficient given the heightened security threat. On 20 April a series of sniping gun attacks took place in Dublin, where Wellington Barracks (present day Griffith College), a Crossley tender on Capel Street, Emmet Dalton's motorcade on Parnell Square, and City Hall were fired upon. According to the *Irish Times*, the 'guards on the City Hall were sniped from the roofs of houses overlooking the building during the night. The guards replied vigorously to the fire, with what result is not known. The Headquarters of the Provisional Government was subjected to a heavy fire from various points in the locality'.

31

With the start of the civil war in late June, the workings of the military and the Provisional government underwent profound changes, with the whole government focusing almost exclusively on the military situation. Collins became commander-in-chief of the army, Fionan Lynch became vice-commandant of the south-western division, Kevin O'Higgins became assistant Adjutant General, and Joseph McGrath became Director of Intelligence. City Hall became no longer a site of government but more of a site of war. In fact, the National Army of the Irish Free State took over City Hall from the day the civil war broke out in Dublin on 28 June until 19 July 1923. Immediately after the war started, the National Army issued a call to arms, with generous pay and allowances on offer for those who enlisted in the force. From then on, hundreds of people queued outside City Hall seeking to join the National Army.

Soon City Hall became a site of mourning as the two leading figures of the pro-Treaty side, Griffith and Collins died within 10 days of each other in August 1922. After Griffith died in his home on 12 August, his body was moved to City Hall the following day where it lay in state in the Central Hall, which was draped in black. An almost unending stream of mourners passed through the hall to pay their respects before Griffith's body was moved to the Pro-Cathedral before burial at Glasnevin Cemetery.

The same sombre process was repeated all over again days later after Collins was killed in Béal na Bláth in Cork on 22 August. His body was transported by boat from Cork to Dublin, transferred to St. Vincent's Hospital before being moved to City Hall where it lay in state for two days from 24 August. Queues stretched more than a mile long as citizens stood for hours on rain-soaked streets to wait their turn to file past the coffin. Despite City Hall being open from early morning, people were still passing the coffin at midnight. The Provisional Government designated the day of his funeral, Monday 28 August, as a day of mourning in Dublin, with a complete cessation of work other than essential services. Thousands lined the streets as Collins's body was moved from City Hall to the Pro-Cathedral before his burial in Glasnevin. After Griffith and Collins died, the dual system of government came to an end shortly afterwards when both the Dáil and the Provisional governments were fused together when

Michael Collins' funeral procession
courtesy of Dublin City Library and Archives

Sean Collins Mourns as Michael Collins Lies in State in City Hall
courtesy of National Library of Ireland

the Third Dáil met for the first time on 9 September, with W.T. Cosgrave becoming chairperson of the amalgamated government. City Hall was replaced as government headquarters by newly erected buildings in Upper Merrion Street in July, which partly housed the Royal College of Science, the Department of Agriculture, with a third section being taken over by the government.

Dublin City Hall, which had played such a significant role in 1922 as the provisional government's headquarters as it attempted to embark on statehood, finally returned into the hands of Dublin Corporation. The Corporation took over full control of Dublin City Hall in the second half of 1923 for the first time since it was taken over by British Authorities in December 1920. And just as it sought and received compensation from the British government for occupying the building, Dublin Corporation sought compensation of up to £4,000 from the Free State government and the Irish Army for damage done to the building during their occupation and the renovation needed to enable the Corporation staff to use the location again.

Further Reading:

- Minutes of Dublin Corporation 1922-1923, Dublin City Library and Archive

- *Dublin City Hall restored.* History Ireland, Vol. 8, No. 2 (Summer 2000)

- *History of Dublin City Hall.* Dublin City Council Website, available at https://www.dublincity.ie/residential/arts-and-events/city-hall/history-city-hall.

- Second Dáil – 2nd Ministry (Post Treaty). Government of Ireland Website, available at https://www.gov.ie/ga/foilsiuchan/99eec5-second-dail/#second-dail-2nd-ministry-post-treaty.

- Dublin City Libraries subscribes to the *Irish Times* Newspaper Archive and the Irish Newspaper Archives Online, which give access to a searchable electronic archive of newspaper titles in the city's libraries.

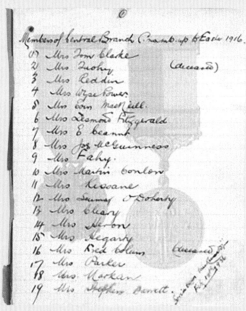

Mrs. Margaret 'Loo' Kennedy's record of Cumann na mBan members in Dublin courtesy of Military Service Pensions Collection

Women activists in Dublin during the Civil War

Mary Muldowney, Historian in Residence, Dublin Central

Following the enrolment of women in the Irish Citizen Army in 1913 and the formation of Cumann na mBan in 1914, female republicans were eager to carry arms and take the same risks as their male comrades. Cumann na mBan had been founded on 2 April 1914 as an auxiliary body to assist the Irish Volunteers. Their status elicited some criticism from feminist women, who felt they should have insisted on equality. During the 1916 Rising women were usually confined to cooking, first aid, messaging and signalling duties in support of male combatants, although there were some notable exceptions who participated in the fighting.

During the War of Independence, although they were still forbidden from fighting on the battlefield, Republican women were at risk of serious injury from their encounters with the British Forces. At least two Cumann na mBan members from Dublin – Josephine (Josie) McGowan and Margaret Keogh were killed during the struggle. Cumann na mBan was at its strongest, in terms of numbers and the commitment of the members, when the Truce took place in July 1921.

The Treaty debates in the Dáil lasted fifteen days, with a break for Christmas, and they were held in both public and private sessions. The private sessions were held on 15-17 December and on the morning of 6 January. Details of the private sessions were not released to the public until the early 1970s because of concern about the divisive nature of contributions and personal attacks made by members against their colleagues.

In the first half of 1922 the Sinn Féin cabinet, the second Dáil, the IRA and the electorate exercised their opinions on the Treaty in that order. As the divisions deepened, they also became harder to bridge. There was scope for compromise, as Michael Collins and Éamon de Valera, as leaders of the two sides, were divided by temperament and experience, not by ideology, but attitudes hardened as the months passed.

Some of the worst invective in the public sessions was levelled against the six women TDs who were opposed to the Treaty. These were Ada English, Constance Markievicz, Kathleen Clarke, Kathleen O'Callaghan, Mary McSwiney and Margaret Pearse. They were dismissed by many of their male colleagues as being merely the relatives of dead heroes but they were elected in their own right and had very definite opinions about the Treaty that were far from being inherited from their male relatives. The Oath of Allegiance was mentioned repeatedly in their speeches, when they said they could never betray the earlier Oath they had sworn in 1916, to the Irish Republic.

During this transition phase, pro-Treaty leaders acted in the name of both the Provisional Government and the Second Dáil, thus bolstering their popular legitimacy. However, from an early stage, the new regime faced deep opposition from within the Irish Republican Army (IRA). Éamon de Valera resigned as president and Arthur Griffith was elected by a majority of two votes. De Valera and the 57 deputies who had voted against the Treaty formed a new political group called Cumann na Poblachta (Republic Party).

At a special convention of the membership on 5 February 1922 Cumann na mBan became the first major organisation to reject the Treaty, by 419 votes to 63. Pro-Treaty members formed a new organisation, Cumann na Saoirse, to support the Free State government. Two of the founding members of Cumann na mBan, Jenny Wyse-Power and Alice Stopford-Green were among those leading the new group. Cumann na Saoirse collaborated with the National Army and the former comrades from both organisations spied on each other once the fighting began.

Women were allowed to play a fuller military role during the Civil War than had been the case in the War of Independence. John Borgonovo's chapter in *Women and the Irish Revolution* argues that the gradual defeat of the anti-Treaty IRA created the conditions for the members of Cumann na mBan to take on greater military responsibilities than they had during the War of Independence period. One of their most visible and potentially dangerous duties was to provide the military honours at the funerals of anti-Treaty Republicans. Cumann na mBan members had taken part in some major funeral processions in the previous years, like that of Thomas Ashe and Muriel (Gifford) MacDonagh, which had significant propaganda value and also helped to build public support for the independence struggle. The Free State Government proved to be much tougher in their attitude to women who opposed the Treaty than the British authorities had been to female revolutionaries.

On 14 April, Rory O'Connor led 200 anti-Treaty IRA men under his command in an occupation of the Four Courts, in total defiance of the Provisional Government of the Irish Free State. It became the headquarters of the most uncompromising IRA leaders, including Liam Mellows, Ernie O'Malley and Oscar Traynor.

On the pro-Treaty side of the IRA, Collins was followed by the majority of his headquarters staff, who had been in Dublin with him through most of the War of Independence. Although several of the Dublin divisions opted for the anti-Treaty position, members of the Squad and the Active Service Units followed Collins, possibly out of personal loyalty as much as any belief in the Free State.

Jenny Wyse-Power and Alice Stopford-Green courtesy of Wikimedia Commons

Six women TDs who opposed the Treaty. Clockwise from top left:
Ada English, Constance Markievicz, Kathleen Clarke,
Mary McSwiney, Margaret Pearse and Kathleen O'Callaghan
courtesy of Wikimedia Commons

The British Army still had thousands of soldiers concentrated in Dublin, awaiting evacuation. Winston Churchill, the Secretary of State for the Colonies in the British Cabinet, urged Collins to ensure that the force was ejected from the Four Courts, claiming it was a breach of the Treaty and in contempt of the law. Facing sustained IRA opposition to their governing authority and the threatened British reoccupation of the country, Free State ministers saw no alternative to military action. The British army had 6,000 troops still stationed in Dublin alone and Churchill was pushing for them to be deployed against the occupiers of the Four Courts. The Provisional Government authorised a National Army assault on the Four Courts to begin on the night of 27/28 June 1922, using borrowed British army weaponry.

Cathal Brugha was shot outside the Hammam Hotel in Sackville Street (O'Connell Street) in the final hours of the Battle for Dublin in July 1922. Cumann na mBan member Linda Kearns, a trained nurse, held his severed artery as he was driven to the Mater Hospital. On 7th July 1922 he died in

Destruction of Hammam Hotel, Sackville Street, 1922
courtesy of Dublin City Libraries Flickr album, The Civil War in Dublin

the Mater Hospital, suffering from the after effects of a major bullet wound to his leg. The bitterness between former comrades is evident in the open letter published by his widow Caitlin, herself a member of Cumann na mBan. She insisted that Cumann na mBan members provide the honour guard.

Another prominent anti-Treaty man was shot by Free State forces in a hotel room in Skerries in August 1922. Harry Boland was on the run. Cumann na mBan member Eileen McCarville (nee McGrane) gave an account of the funeral in her Witness Statement to the Bureau of Military History:

> At the funeral Cumann na mBan took charge as the men did not appear. Sighle Humphries and I were in charge and walked at the head of the cortege to Glasnevin. There were several bands playing the dead march on the route. It was very solemn and sad and left on me an unforgettable impression.

In September 1922, prompted by the killing of Michael Collins in the previous month, the Provisional Government proposed the establishment of military courts to try those who persisted in their armed resistance to the Anglo-Irish Treaty. The Army Emergency Powers Bill was passed by the Dáil on 27 September 1922 and gave the power to military courts to punish by death, imprisonment or deportation those found guilty of attacks on the army, the destruction of property or the unauthorised possession of arms. The first four executions were carried out in Dublin in November 1922.

A decision was taken by the Prisoners Department of the Provisional Government to use the hospital section of B Wing in Mountjoy Military Prison to hold female prisoners. On 9 November, the headquarters of the anti-Treaty Cumann na Poblachta party was raided by Irish Free State troops and all those found on the premises were arrested. This included ten women who were arrested and sent to Mountjoy Jail. The Deputy Governor O'Keeffe always dealt with women prisoners.

At this point B Wing was holding thirty women; comprising nineteen political and eleven criminal prisoners. The convict prisoners were there to clean the wing and serve the food to the political prisoners. There were also female warders working there. A decision was taken by the Prisons

Department to use the hospital section of B Wing in Mountjoy Military Prison to hold female prisoners. At the end of November political prisoner status was granted which enabled the prisoners to wear their own clothes and accept responsibility for cooking and serving their food. They were also required to keep their quarters clean. However, in Mountjoy the women refused to clean the general area of their block, drawing the line at their own cells.

The matron arranged for some of the criminal prisoners to be brought in to 'clean up the place.' Historian Ann Matthews said that the interned women appeared to believe they should be allowed to select the aspects of the political prisoner regulations that suited them, unlike the male political prisoners in other jails, who followed the rules. Many female political prisoners came from comfortable backgrounds and they had employed servants and charwomen. As Matthews said, they had never wielded a mop or broom in their own homes. The records of the women interned between 1922 and 1923 indicate that the prisoners came predominantly from more affluent areas. Few residents from the slum areas of Dublin City were imprisoned.

During the period of the Civil War and for several months following the Arms Dump that ended it, female political prisoners were held at Mountjoy Jail, Kilmainham Jail, and the hospital compound in the North Dublin Union, which had been used as a British Army barracks in the War of Independence. In each of the three prisons, the women elected a prisoners' council whose role was to deal with the authorities but also to exert discipline, even though not all of the prisoners were members of Cumann na mBan.

Maud Gonne McBride and Charlotte Despard had formed the Women Prisoners' Defence League in August 1922. It was an anti-Free State association whose sole remit was to protest at the imprisonment of anti Treatyites. Between November 1922 and November 1923, twenty-four hunger strikes took place in the three female prisons, in which a total of 219 women took part. The first hunger strike took place in November 1922 when Mary McSwiney was incarcerated in Mountjoy Jail and went on hunger strike as a protest against her imprisonment. Every Sunday the

HUNGER-STRIKING OUTSIDE MOUNTJOY PRISON IN SYMPATHY WITH HER SISTER WITHIN: MISS ANNIE McSWINEY (SECOND FROM RIGHT) NEXT TO MRS. DESPARD (EXTREME RIGHT).

Annie McSwiney and Charlotte Despard outside Mountjoy Prison courtesy of National Museum of Ireland, museum.ie

Women Prisoners' Defence League held public meetings at the gates of Mountjoy where they denounced the government on McSwiney's behalf and McBride told the assembled crowd 'to protest against the attempt to murder the sister of Terence McSwiney' adding 'this infamous Government should be wiped out.' Annie McSwiney joined the fray by sitting outside the gates of Mountjoy Jail, going on hunger strike in solidarity with her sister.

The Military Service Pension files are one of the best sources for finding information about the role of women during the revolutionary period. For instance, when I used the most basic search terms 'Cumann na mBan' and 'funeral' the database identified 183 applicants who mentioned attendance at funerals, whether participating in the cortege, providing an escort or being a member of an honour guard as an element of their service in Cumann na mBan. Of that number, 49 were from Dublin. The organisation was excluded from the 1924 Military Service Pensions Act but included after the 1934 Act was passed. One of the most appealing aspects of the application files is that they contain the women's own accounts of their activities, together with the references from commanding officers and others who could vouch for them. Here are some brief outlines of typical applications for military service pensions by Dublin women who served in Cumann na mBan in 1916, the War of Independence and the Civil War:

ROSE WILLIAMSON was branch secretary of the Eamonn Ceannt branch of the Dublin Brigade of Cumann na mBan. Following the outbreak of the Civil War on 28 June 1922 she was on first aid duty in Earl Street, Dublin, and cooked food for anti-Treaty IRA forces fighting in that area as well as helping to distribute the 'War News' publication. She was one of the Guard of Honour at the lying-in-state of Cathal Brugha; she attended Harry Boland's funeral, helped to store some arms and took part in demonstrations demanding the release of Republican prisoners during the Civil War.

Rose's sister **Margaret Hewett (nee Williamson)** was also a member of the Eamonn Ceannt branch of Cumann na mBan. She was on active duty at the Earl Street dispensary during the week of fighting in June 1922 and the early days of July and during the initial Four Courts attack she helped to commandeer food for the garrison from the area around Fleet Street, Aston Quay and Dame Street. Margaret also transported firearms to Volunteers on duty at the Earl Street dispensary; distributed copies of 'War News' around the city from 27 Dawson Street; took part in the Guard of Honour at the lying-in-state of Cathal Brugha; paraded at the funerals of Cathal Brugha and Harry Boland and carried arms and ammunition from Bishop Street to Dawson Street for an attack on Jury's Hotel.

Cumann na mBan members hold hands for crowd control at
Cathal Brugha funeral in Dublin, July 1922 courtesy of RTÉ Archives

Sheila Daly (nee Curran) was a member of the Central Branch. On the outbreak of the Civil War she was instructed to go to 44 Parnell Square where she remained until she was moved again to Jenkins' of Capel Street where escapees from the Four Courts were hiding. While at Parnell Square, she took messages to outposts, and assisted wherever possible. In Capel Street, she cooked and assisted the men even while the building was being attacked and under fire. She returned to Parnell Square when Jenkins' was evacuated, from which she went to the post at the Duke of Leinster's house, and when that was evacuated she assisted in bringing guns from outposts and dumping them in McMahon's, in Dominick Lane. Following this she returned home, did dispatch duty and called to 32, North Great George's Street nightly for several months for dispatches; attended public funerals and remained active until the end of this period. Her application for a pension was also successful.

Lil Kearns was another member of the Central branch. She took up garrison duty on 28 June at 44 Parnell Square and helped to transport arms. After the evacuation of this outpost, she took several guns back to 44 Parnell Square and remained there until 2 July 1922 when she brought four revolvers to Sullivan Street, North Circular Road. Under the command of Lily McClean and Eilis Ryan, she transported arms from the home of Miss Mary Scully, 39 St. Patrick's Road, Drumcondra to a stable in Montague Lane; transported ammunition from St. Columba's Road to another location; carried two guns with Sheila Brennan from a house in Summerhill Place to the Black Church for an IRA operation and carried them back; aided the desertion of four National Army soldiers from Mountjoy Prison with their arms and ammunition and brought them to 131 Morehampton Road. She attended the funeral of Cathal Brugha. Lil Kearns was arrested on 02 May 1923 and interned in Kilmainham and North Dublin Union until 20 September 1923. She said that her brother died during this period and she was offered release if she would sign the form committing to the Free State but she refused. Lil's pension application was successful but she was refused a gratuity for a disease or wound, despite the hardships she suffered while imprisoned in the North Dublin Union, including being forced to sleep out in the open for three weeks in May 1923.

ERNIE O'MALLEY wrote in *The Singing Flame*, his memoir of the Civil War, that as the death toll mounted, the unenviable task of burying the dead with full military honours was undertaken by Cumann na mBan. He described how the women, 'with eyes shut and faces screwed to one side, fired a volley over the graves with revolvers or automatics'. While this might be taken to mean that he was mocking the women, during the Civil War he learned to appreciate their bravery and to regret that they had never had 'sufficient status' in previous conflicts. He described them as 'loyal, willing and incorruptible comrades'. Despite the role played by Cumann na mBan and female Irish Citizen Army members, and the contributions of so many women who belonged to other groups or were not members of an organisation at all, successive Irish governments refused to recognise their right to equal citizenship. Subsequent decades not only saw the promises in the 1916 Proclamation of the Republic being broken but laws were passed that curtailed women's access to employment and public service. When the fiftieth anniversary commemoration of the 1916 Rising took place, women were scarcely mentioned at all but the Decade of Commemorations that commenced in 2012 has overturned that omission.

Further reading

- CONNOLLY, LINDA (ED)., *Women and the Irish Revolution* (Irish Academic Press, 2020)

- CROWLEY, JOHN, Ó DRISCEOIL, DONAL, MURPHY, MIKE (EDS.), BORGONOVO, JOHN (ASSOCIATE ED.), *Atlas of the Irish Revolution*, Cork University Press, 2017)

- GILLIS, LIZ, *Women of the Irish Revolution* (Mercier Press,

- MATTHEWS, ANN, *Renegades, Irish Republican Women 1900-1922* (Mercier Press, 2014)

- MCCARTHY, CAL, *Cumann na mBan and the Irish Revolution* (The Collins Press, 2007)

Websites

- Bureau of Military History Witness Statements: https://www.militaryarchives.ie/collections/online-collections/bureau-of-military-history-1913-1921

- Military Service Pension Applications: https://www.militaryarchives.ie/collections/online-collections/military-service-pensions-collection-1916-1923/search-the-collection

caṫal bruġa
A fuair bár ar ron na h-Éireann, ar an
7aṡ lá lúil, 1922

Postcard featuring a photograph of Cathal Brugha in Irish Volunteer
uniform published after his death on 7 July 1922
courtesy of Dublin City Library and Archive

Remembering Cathal Brugha

James Curry, Historian in Residence,
Dublin North West Area

In December 1918 Cathal Brugha stood as a Sinn Féin election candidate, with a contemporary handbill introducing him to voters in his selected constituency of Waterford County as:

> *One of the leading spirits in the Irish Ireland Movements during the past 15 years ... a fluent Irish Speaker and Scholar, an Officer of the Irish Volunteers, and a member of the Sinn Féin Executive.*

The document went on to say of Brugha that:

> *His coolness, courage and daring in the Rebellion of 1916 have won for him the admiration of all his comrades. Though severely wounded in the fight, he refused to leave his post until he collapsed. The County of Waterford will have in him a Soldier and a Statesman as their Representative.*

Like so many other republican candidates, the 44-year-old Dubliner coasted to victory in that landmark general election, which led to Sinn Féin setting up Dáil Éireann the following month. Brugha secured over 75% of the vote from a constituency that may not have known much about the Dublin commercial traveller, who co-owned a candle making firm at 14 Lower Ormond Quay, but was satisfied, to quote one contemporary, 'when they heard he was a 1916 man, [and] that he carried a few British bullets in him'.

Less than four years later, Brugha became the first high-profile casualty of the Irish Civil War, with the bullet that killed him this time fired by a member of the Free State forces. His memorial mass at Phibsborough's St. Joseph's Church and funeral service at Glasnevin Cemetery attracted a

ÉIRE 24

Statesmen of Ireland

Cathal Brugha

1987

large turnout as Brugha was laid to rest in Glasnevin's Republican Plot, 'between ninety and one hundred priests from city parishes' attending the burial. The previous month, he was re-elected to Dáil Éireann although never received an opportunity of taking his seat.

Cathal Brugha, as he called himself after joining the Gaelic League in his teens and becoming a fluent Irish speaker, was born Charles William St John Burgess on 18 July 1874 at his family home of 13 Richmond Avenue, Fairview, with the birth registered in the district of Coolock and Drumcondra. He was the tenth of fourteen children born to art dealer Thomas Burgess, a Carlow native, and his Dublin wife Marianne (née Flynn), with the household nationalist in outlook. Although Thomas Burgess was a Protestant, all the family's children were raised as Catholics like their mother, and 'young Charles was particularly devout in his religious observances'. Educated at the Colmkille Schools and Belvedere College, Brugha had his schooling cut short due to economic necessity and started work as a clerk for a church supplies firm before becoming a commercial traveller. His father passed away in April 1899, while the family were living at 12 Glenarm Avenue in Drumcondra, leaving behind just £20 in his will.

While living at 36 Cabra Road in Glasnevin, Cathal Brugha filled out his 1911 census return in Irish, and the following year, as Cathal Burgess, married Cathleen Kingston (later Caitlín Brugha). The pair lived in Rathmines at 5

Fitzwilliam Terrace, Dartmouth Road, and had six children over the next decade, five daughters and a son, Ruairí, who later became a Fianna Fáil TD for South County Dublin and married Máire MacSwiney, daughter of Cork republican martyr Terence MacSwiney (1879-1920).

In November 1913 Cathal Brugha joined the newly formed Irish Volunteers and was appointed adjutant of the C Company, 4th Dublin Battalion. During the Easter Rising, his battalion occupied the South Dublin Union, with Brugha serving as Vice-Commandant to Eamonn Ceannt and becoming separated from his unit on Thursday, 27 April, as he held off British soldiers despite suffering numerous bullet and shrapnel wounds. Ceannt subsequently found Brugha 'propped against a wall in a pool of his own blood clutching a pistol as he defiantly sang 'God Save Ireland' and taunted the attacking troops'.

After receiving medical treatment at several hospitals for his wounds, Brugha was discharged in August 1916 and made a partial recovery from his injuries. He would 'continue the reorganisation of Irish resistance' over the next couple of years and played an important role in reviving the Irish Volunteers. From October 1917 to April 1918, Brugha served on the Sinn Féin executive, resigning over the party's cooperation with the Irish Parliamentary Party during the conscription crisis. During this period, Brugha 'travelled to London with a party of twelve Volunteers intent on assassinating British government ministers if conscription were imposed on Ireland ... [and] organising an attack on the British cabinet remained his pet project throughout the War of Independence'.

Elected as acting president (príomh-aire) of Dáil Éireann the day after its first meeting on 21 January 1919, Brugha stepped down a few months later upon Éamon de Valera's return and was appointed as Minister for Defence, 'one of the few leading separatists to remain at large throughout 1918-21, [when] he was often on the run'. In the aftermath of the Truce agreed in July 1921, Brugha 'flatly refused' to go to the talks in London to produce a settlement and was in the west of Ireland along with de Valera and Richard Mulcahy when they heard the news that the Anglo-Irish Treaty had been signed.

Believing the Treaty to be 'national suicide', in January 1922 Brugha launched a bitter personal attack on Michael Collins, whom he had endured a strained relationship with for several years, describing him as 'merely a subordinate in the Department of Defence' and rubbishing Arthur Griffith's characterisation of Collins as 'the man who won the war'. After the narrow ratification of the Treaty by the Dáil, Brugha was replaced as Minister for Defence by Richard Mulcahy, and although he sought to avoid civil war, when the fighting broke out with the shelling of the Four Courts on 28 June 1922, Brugha 'reported for duty to the Hammam Hotel in Upper O'Connell Street, which with the Gresham and Granville hotels had been taken over by anti-treatyites'.

On 5 July, after the area had come under heavy fire and the buildings left untenable, Brugha refused to surrender and upon emerging from Thomas Lane, was shot in the left thigh with the bullet severing his femoral artery. A Cumann na mBan member named Linda Kearns kept 'her fingers on his severed artery to stem the loss of blood' but following an operation which initially seemed successful, Brugha died two days later at the Mater Hospital on 7 July 1922, aged 47. A military inquest concluded that he died from 'Shock and Haemorrhage caused by a bullet fired by a person unknown'.

Cathal Brugha's gravestone at Glasnevin Cemetery
courtesy of James Curry

'As a protest against the "immediate and terrible" Civil War made by the so-called Provisional Government on the Irish Republican Forces', Cathal's widow Caitlín issued a statement to the press, requesting that 'apart from

Photograph of Caitlín Brugha, taken in September 1923 at Kilbrien, Co. Waterford courtesy of Waterford County Museum

family relations and intimate friends, the chief mourners and the Guard of Honour should include only the women of the Republican movement'. Asking that 'the representatives of the Free State or its officials' do not attend the funeral; she made a point of ending her statement by noting that 'this does not exclude the general public from attending'. It was thus members of Cumann na mBan who acted as guards of honour when Cathal Brugha lay in state at the Mater Hospital for two days, and during the funeral itself on 10 July 1922, when the coffin was draped in the tricolour flag.

After becoming a widow at the age of forty-three with six young children, Caitlín Brugha, a native of County Offaly who 'shared her husband's ardent republicanism and supported his activities', carried on her spouse's work in various ways, including as a politician. Strongly opposed to the Anglo-Irish Treaty, she topped the poll as a Sinn Féin TD for Waterford City and

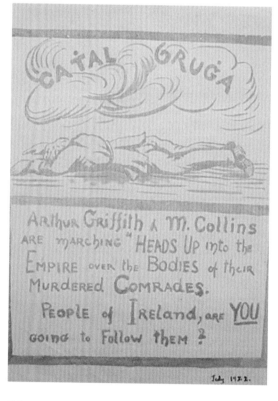

Irish Civil War mimeograph print featuring a depiction of Cathal Brugha's fatal shooting in July 1922, an artwork attributed to Constance Markievicz courtesy of Capuchin Archives, Ireland

County in the Free State's August 1923 election and was re-elected as a Sinn Féin TD to the short-lived Fifth Dáil four years later.

Following Cathal Brugha's death, efforts were made to ensure that he was remembered as a martyr who died fighting for an Irish Republic he had helped to establish in 1916. For example, during the Irish Civil War, a hard-hitting artwork that has been attributed to Constance Markievicz depicted the death of Cathal Brugha on a mimeograph print with some accompanying text. There are at least three different versions of this artwork, all depicting Brugha's prone and bloody body beneath explosive clouds hanging over Ireland as the long-threatened civil war finally came to pass.

The accompanying text in one version declared that Michael Collins and Arthur Griffith were marching heads up into the British Empire over the bodies of their murdered comrades, and then asked the 'People of Ireland, are you going to follow them?' Another version was addressed to members of the Free State's National Army, with the text reading:

> *The murder of Cathal Brugha has dishonoured the Free State uniforms. Men in Green, throw them off and cease to do England's dirty work!*

A third variation was again addressed to members of the National Army, with the text reading:

> *Men in Green. Throw off the Green Tunics that have been dishonoured.*

Interestingly, in this contemporary depiction of Brugha's death the subject appears defenceless. It is accepted that Brugha was armed when he refused to halt and surrender to Free State troops after coming out of the burning buildings on O'Connell Street. Indeed, in at least one account, it is stated that Brugha held a revolver in each hand. In the next day's issue of the *Irish Independent*, under the headlines 'Mr. Brugha's Dash. Cry of 'Halt' Unheeded', it is stated that:

It was when the firemen were battering down one of the doors that a small man, dust-begrimed, with a drawn revolver in each hand, sprang forward. A Red Cross man appealed to him, for God's sake, to stop.

'No no,' he replied, and on he went towards Findlator's Place, and calls of "Halt!" could be heard amid the roar of the flames; but the man, who was Mr. Cathal Brugha, paid no heed to his command. A volley of shots rang out, and Mr. Brugha fell, blood spurting from his wound, and his weapons fell from his grasp. He made a desperate effort to rise, but again fell back. Doctors and Red Cross nurses rushed to the injured man, and, having dressed the wound, he was removed to hospital in an ambulance.

After the death of Cathal Brugha, Michael Collins is said to have remarked, despite the pair's difficult relationship, that:

'Because of his sincerity, I would forgive him anything. At worst he was a fanatic – though in what had been a noble cause. At best I remember him amongst the very few who gave their all that this country should have its freedom. When many of us are forgotten, Cathal Brugha will be remembered'.

Yet, by 1929 Sinn Féin's Austin Stack, a Dáil Éireann cabinet minister from November 1919 until the ratification of the Anglo-Irish Treaty, was quoted as saying:

'I think that Cathal Brugha, whom I regard as one of the greatest figures amongst all those who have been connected with the fight for freedom, is not sufficiently known to the Irish people'.

To help combat this situation and keep Brugha's memory alive, numerous books or studies have been written since the 1940s. Twenty years after his death, Brugha's 'friend and political ally', journalist and Irish language activist J.J. O'Kelly, writing under the pseudonym Sceilg, published a substantial biography entitled *Cathal Brugha le Seán MaCealaigh*. Written in old Irish script (cló Gaelach), this 1942 work contains valuable details and insights about Brugha's life and has been described as 'typical of the historiography of this period: reverent, hagiographical and overtly nationalist'. Five years later, the same author included an English language account of Brugha's life, focused mainly 'on the period from the Truce until his death almost exactly a year later', in his book *A Trinity of Martyrs: Terence MacSwiney, Cathal Brugha, Austin Stack*, which is 'infused with his own particular political stance'.

In 1955 a short pamphlet about Brugha's life was published by Sinn Féin's Brian Dillon Branch in Cork City, and fourteen years later, his nephew Tomás Ó Dochartaigh published a hagiographical biography written in Irish called *Cathal Brugha: A Shaol is a Thréithe*. Drawing upon the earlier research of Sceilg, this is 'a shorter though more focused account of Brugha's life'. In April 1966, Major Florence O'Donoghue, Cork Irish Volunteers No.1 Brigade intelligence officer during the War of Independence, delivered a lecture on Brugha's life and times which played down the subject's feud with Michael Collins and ignored 'Brugha's audacious plans of political assassination' in his final years. Brugha's son Ruairí, who told O'Donoghue he was 'never satisfied with the Sceilg book from an objective point of view', had hoped that the lecture would be published, although this wish went unfilled, with O'Donoghue passing away in December 1967. A transcript of the lecture is, however, contained in O'Donoghue's personal papers held by the National Library of Ireland.

Another lecture about Brugha, delivered by Micheál Ó Cillín to the Old Dublin Society in 1985, was published in the organisation's *Dublin Historical Record* journal later that year. And twenty years later, an 'understandably favourable' biographical sketch of Brugha by his grandson of the same name was included in Máire MacSwiney Brugha's memoir *History's Daughter*. The author of this biographical piece had previously performed on stage as his namesake uncle during a commemorative pageant at Dublin's Olympia Theatre in July 1972 to mark the fiftieth anniversary of Brugha's death, written and produced by Noel Mannix and noted by a contemporary theatre critic for its 'fervid patriotic aura and … utter devotion to its subject'.

In 2018 Fergus O'Farrell's concise and informative biography *Cathal Brugha* was published, drawing heavily on Bureau of Military History archival sources, and building upon the author's MA thesis to challenge the simplistic portrayal of its subject as 'a strong advocate of violence' who was distrustful of politics and instead present him as a figure who 'sought to marry force with politics in the pursuit of Irish independence'. During the summer of 2022 the centenary of Brugha's death was marked by the publication of Daithí Ó Corráin and Gerard Hanley's *Cathal Brugha: 'An Indomitable Spirit'*, a full-length biographical study that provides 'a broad and multifaceted portrait of a complex, tenacious, and often maligned figure'.

Other efforts to commemorate Brugha on the centenary of his death included the installation of temporary placards at Cathedral Street near the site of his fatal shooting by a group called Independent Dublin Republicans, part of a collection remembering 'Republican Heroes' that have been erected across the city in recent times.

Nearby, Cathal Brugha is remembered with the naming of Cathal Brugha Street, as well as the 'Áras Brugha' building at the former headquarters of the National Health Insurance Company at 9-10 Upper O'Connell Street (named in 1934 despite the objections of his widow), which carries a circular bronze relief plaque featuring a bas-relief image of Brugha. Elsewhere in the city, Portobello Barracks in Rathmines has been renamed Cathal Brugha Barracks since 1952.

Temporary placard and wreath erected at Cathedral Street in July 2022 to mark the centenary of Cathal Brugha's death, erected by "Independent Dublin Republicans" courtesy of James Curry

The Funeral of Harry Boland by Jack B. Yeats
courtesy of The Model. Home of the Niland Collection, Sligo

Street sign for Cathal Brugha Street in Dublin courtesy of James Curry

After his death, Cathal Brugha – an uncompromising republican who 'did not encourage discussion and gave his opinions with directness and finality' – was described by Harry Boland, another anti-treaty Sinn Féin TD who would be killed during the opening months of the Irish Civil War, as 'easily the greatest man of his day'. At his personal request, Boland was buried next to Brugha at Glasnevin Cemetery's Republican Plot in August 1922.

Also buried at Glasnevin in December 1959 was Caitlín Brugha, who after her husband's death became a founder and managing director of Kingston's Ltd drapery business which operated several branches in Dublin, including one at 'Hammam Buildings, Upper O'Connell St., at the rear of which [Cathal] Brugha was killed shortly after the outbreak of the Civil War'.

Further Reading:

- MacSwiney Brugha, Máire. *History's Daughter. A Memoir from the only child of Terence MacSwiney.* O'Brien Press, 2005

- Ó Corráin, Daithí & Hanley, Gerard. *Cathal Brugha: 'An Indomitable Spirit'.* Four Courts Press, 2022

- O'Farrell, Fergus. *Cathal Brugha.* UCD Press, 2018

- Quinn, James. 'Brugha, Cathal'. *Dictionary of Irish Biography.* https://www.dib.ie/biography/brugha-cathal-a1077

A History workshop for children with Dublin City Council Culture Company
courtesy of Dublin City Council Culture Company

'It's part of who we are today'. Children making sense of the Civil War

Dervilia Roche, Historian in Residence for Children

The year 2022 has seen a variety of talks, performances and other events that have marked the 100 year anniversary of the beginning of the Irish Civil War, helping us all to understand and remember this complex time in Irish history. Included in these events were history workshops for children about the opening days and weeks of the Civil War in Dublin, designed to provide some clarity on this huge topic to children, to help them to understand the historical events and indeed the commemorations happening throughout the year.

Since September 2020, I have been working as the Historian in Residence for Children based out of Richmond Barracks, as part of Dublin City Council Culture Company's Creative Residency programme. This residency is made in partnership with Dublin City Libraries, and involves working with children aged 9 to 12 across the city, through history workshops, projects, summer camps, and more. These activities aim to bring history to life for children, to help them uncover their own local and social history, and to further their curiosity and explorations of Dublin and history in general.

While the workshops and projects cover a wide range of historical topics, many of them have related to historical wars, from the world wars to those of Ireland's revolutionary history, with a focus this year on the Civil War events in Dublin. I have learned from the children I've worked with how much of an interest there is in topics like these among young people, but also the challenges and responsibilities we have in helping children explore these darker sides of history.

Why talk to children about war?

Since taking up the role of Historian in Residence for Children in 2020, some of the topics I have talked to children about include the Irish Civil War, as well as the Easter Rising, the Irish War of Independence, the Anglo-Irish Treaty and many more. The topics and themes that my workshops are based on are all drawn from consulting with children about their interests and curiosities. It has been clear throughout the residency that there is a real interest among children in military history. Sometimes this stems from an interest in understanding how wars and battles originate or in understanding what life is like during wartime. For children in the 9 to 12 age group, there is a wealth of historical fiction books set during the world wars, and this has been a starting point for many children's interests.

In terms of the Irish Civil War, many of the children I have worked with have been curious to find out more about it, having heard of it but not really having a clear understanding or complete knowledge. They are sometimes more likely to know more about and talk more about civil wars in other countries. In several workshops on related topics, children have asked me "What was the Irish Civil War about?" and asked about comparisons between the numbers of people involved in, and the numbers of people who died in the various turbulent stages of the Irish revolutionary period.

The 100 year anniversary of the beginning of the Irish Civil War in 2022 was an opportunity to address this curiosity, and the workshops formed part of a wider programme of events run with the other Historians in Residence. It was also an opportunity to help children to have a fuller understanding of other commemorations of the war going on during the year, and to make it easier for them to engage in and participate in those activities.

Understanding the divisions and tensions of the past can of course help us to move forward and to ensure the same mistakes are not made again. It can also help children to make sense of current events around the world where fighting is taking place, and to make sense of the ways modern Ireland is still shaped by the legacy of the war. For many children, understanding the war may even mean discovering and understanding personal or family connections to those events.

Explosion at the Four Courts. Images and video footage
are effective tools for encouraging engagement
courtesy of Dublin City Library and Archive

Ways to approach it

It can be challenging to talk to children about war, in a way that is
appropriate, ethical, informative, and responsive to their curiosities.
As with all aspects of history, an important aspect is avoiding bias.
With something like the Irish Civil War, we know that for many people
in Ireland this is still a divisive topic, which may be an influence on
children's views of it. The role of the history workshops is to focus on
the evidence we have as historians, to help the children to access and
understand that evidence, encourage them to think critically about it,
and of course to listen to their opinions. We can try to view the events
of the past with empathy, and to discuss cultural differences between
then and now, and how this might have affected people's behaviour in
the past. Children might strongly identify with the ideas associated with

No. 6.

Means to an End !

The Anti-Treatyites are fond of voting **the dead who died for Ireland !**

And invariably they vote them **against** the Treaty !

If Collins, Mulcahy, etc., had died they would be voted "Anti" also !!

Listen to Padraig Pearse himself :—

"The fact that Thomas Davis would have accepted and worked on with Repeal in no wise derogates from his status as a Separatist, any more than the fact that many of US would have accepted Home Rule (or even Devolution) and worked on with it derogates from OUR status as Separatists. Home Rule to US would have been a means to an end. Repeal to Davis would have been a means to an end."

("*The Spiritual Nation*"—P. H. PEARSE.)

VOTE FOR THE TREATY !

Treaty posters. Pro and anti-treaty posters are great prompts for discussion and debate courtesy of Dublin City Library and Archive

WHAT IS AN IRREGULAR ?

An Irregular is one who fights without Pay for the Old Cause which will never die.

WHAT IS A NATIONAL SOLDIER?

A National Soldier is one who fights to establish an English king and an English Constitution in Ireland.

one side of a war, or even with both sides at the same time, and these are all things that can be explored in a workshop through listening and discussion. A really effective activity with these kinds of topics is using group discussion, particularly discussion and debate among the children themselves. In this way, they work together to co-create ideas and meaning from historical subjects that can otherwise be difficult to make sense of, like historical war. Backed up by the evidence and facts we have studied, the children can explore the various perspectives of the people involved in war, and together develop their understanding.

Another way to encourage reflection and critical thinking about a topic like war is to discuss the idea of commemorating history. By asking children questions like "Should we commemorate this part of history? How should we commemorate it?", we encourage them to reflect on the legacy and modern-day relevance of historical events. It allows them to think about what parts of history they feel are important to them, and then to take these ideas and creatively think about new types of commemoration activities that they feel would be appropriate.

Battle of Dublin workshops

As part of the wider programme of events from Dublin City Council to mark the 100 year anniversary of the Irish Civil War, I ran history workshops for children in both school and family groups. I decided to focus the workshops almost entirely on what is sometimes known as "The Battle of Dublin". This name usually refers to the occupation of the Four Courts, the shelling of those buildings, and the subsequent fighting in the O'Connell St area between late June and early July 1922. We used both the involvement of local places in Dublin, as well as the significant anniversary of the battle, as some of the ways for the children to connect with the topic.

We focused the workshops on a timeline activity, matching images and descriptions of events with dates along a timeline. This kind of activity works well to encourage children to begin thinking about the order of

69

The Four Courts. Modern-day photos can help children realise they are often already familiar with the places involved courtesy of Wikimedia Commons

events, much of which can be figured out from the images, even if they have little prior knowledge of the history topic. Gradually, then, it becomes possible to put together the entire story and its sequence of events, even with a complicated story like this one, involving many people and events. After matching up the images with the dates, we discussed each point on the timeline, and in doing so gradually made our way through the story of the Battle of Dublin.

Throughout this, we could fill in details of the story, which for some children can be much more interesting than looking at the bigger picture of the war. We talked about stories of individual people, and how for many people their close friendships and families became divided during

Armoured car. Children often enjoy focussing on the smaller details of war, such as the types of vehicles and weapons used courtesy of National Library of Ireland

the war. We also looked at images of things like armoured cars and the types of weapons used. We looked at modern-day photographs of the places involved, as well as historical ones, to help everyone recognise the buildings and streets that played a part during the war.

Throughout the workshop, there were several points where we could have more in-depth discussion. One example was when looking at pro-treaty and anti-treaty posters. These work well as they are so visual in nature, but also raise questions about propaganda that allow the children to reflect on their own opinions and attitudes. Similarly, after discussing the main points of the Anglo-Irish Treaty, the children could reflect on how they might have felt at the time of the Treaty. Some children at

71

this point talked about which side they may have been on, and for what reasons. This led to some debate in the workshop, which in itself was a valuable learning experience.

We focused throughout on the different kinds of sources that we can use as historians to understand the war. In the case of the fighting in and around the Four Courts during the Civil War, there were a significant number of photos and even some video footage recorded, a lot of which can be accessed from various online archives. All of these provide great first-hand materials for children to engage with, as well as providing different types of media for different learning styles among the group. Discussing the burning of the Four Courts is also an opportunity to talk about the huge loss of public records in the destruction of the Treasury building there, and to reflect on what this might mean for us as people exploring history.

Children's responses

Many of the children attending the Civil War workshops had little or no prior knowledge of it. Part of this may be due to the fact that the Civil War doesn't always form a major part of the primary school curriculum and falls under broader strands such as "1916 and the foundation of the state". Some had a good understanding of the events of 1916, which could be used as one of the entry points to understanding the Civil War. The children I spoke with tended to have a much greater prior knowledge of international wars than those that took place in Ireland, and some were interested in drawing comparisons between different wars, and the similarities in how they started.

Children who took part in the Civil War workshops and other workshops related to historical war were often fascinated with imagining what it would have been like to live through those times, saying things like "It would have been scary", "Guns all over Dublin" and on the topic of people photographing the shelling of the Four Courts "I wouldn't

Commemorations. Children often understand the importance and complexity of commemorating war courtesy Wikimedia Commons

have been the one taking all those photos". They were interested in Dublin's role during these major events, asking "Why did everything always happen in Dublin?", and were understandably curious about what life was like for children in wartime, asking "Did children die?" and commenting on how the lives of children during war might have been affected.

As we explored both sides of the Civil War and the Anglo-Irish Treaty, the children were interested in and capable of debating the different arguments, and understanding the various viewpoints. About the Anglo-Irish Treaty, they expressed some of their thoughts, like "It wasn't full independence", "It was the best they could do", "They needed to stay on the side of the English", and "They didn't care about Northern Ireland". In workshops about the Easter Rising, children debated whether or not the rebellion should have happened, with some saying "It shouldn't have happened because no one should have died" and others saying "They had good reason to rebel".

When discussing whether wars and battles should be commemorated, the children I spoke to were very keen that major events like the Civil War should be remembered, noting that "It's part of our history", "It's part of who we are today", and "It's better to remember wars so we know not to make the same mistakes". They felt that commemorations should be fair and balanced, acknowledging all involved, saying "We need to respect both sides". They sometimes thought that more should be done in this way, suggesting "The British government should have also commemorated the Easter Rising in 2016" and "The British people who died on Bloody Sunday should be remembered too".

Further exploring the Irish Civil War

Your local library is a great starting point for helping children to further explore the history of the Irish Civil War, or for children who are more broadly interested in historical wars and battles. As previously mentioned, there is a really wide variety of historical fiction books for this age group on the topics of things like the first and second world wars, and a smaller number set during the Irish revolutionary period, including some about the Irish Civil War.

There are some excellent visual resources that can be used to explain aspects of the Irish Civil War, with the help of a grown-up. These would include some of the maps and other images in the *Atlas of the Irish Revolution*, which are also available as online resources. There are several online archives of historical photos and videos from the time which can be easily accessed also. A recent project also allows us to take a virtual tour of a digitally-recreated Record Treasury building in the Four Courts, which once held many public records and was destroyed during the initial days of the Irish Civil War. If the children already have a sense of a particular person they want to research, they can check records of individual people in various places online, including in the Military Archives. Aside from exploring books and websites, a visit to the National Museum of Ireland at Collins Barracks allows children to get a closer look at objects relating to the Civil War and many other parts of Ireland's military history.

Talking to older family members and family friends can be a really effective way for children to find out more about any family stories or connections to the past. Like many darker chapters in Irish history, the Civil War is not often talked about much within families, and often these stories are not passed down. With the help of a grown-up, children can think about ways to approach this sensitively with older family members.

The children I've worked with have proven to be curious about the wars of the past, how they came to be and how they affected the way of life for so many people. They have also proven to be capable of critiquing the decisions of the past, and considering the multiple viewpoints of the people involved in those decisions. They understand the importance but also complexity of choosing how we commemorate wars, which perhaps suggests the potential for more consultation with young people in developing these kinds of events and activities going forward. As we continue to remember the Irish Civil War of 100 years ago, and draw towards the end of the Decade of Commemorations, it remains to be seen how today's children and subsequent generations will choose to approach these anniversaries, as Ireland continues to move further past those turbulent times in its history.

Further reading

Children's books set during the Irish Civil War:

- FLEGG, AUBREY, *Katie's War*, O'Brien Press, 1997

- GALLAGHER, BRIAN, *Taking Sides*, O'Brien Press, 2011

- MURPHY, PATRICIA, *The Irish Civil War 1922-23: Ava's Diary*, Poolbeg Press Ltd, 2017

Resources that grown-ups can help with:

- *Atlas of the Irish Revolution Resources for Secondary Schools*, https://www.ucc.ie/en/theirishrevolution/collections/atlas-resources-for-schools/

- CROWLEY, JOHN, Ó DRISCEOIL, DONAL, MURPHY, MIKE & BORGONOVO, JOHN, *Atlas of the Irish Revolution*, Cork University Press, 2017

- IFI Archive Player, ifiarchiveplayer.ie

- Military Archives, https://www.militaryarchives.ie

- Virtual Treasury, https://virtualtreasury.ie

About Historians in Residence

Since 2017, Dublin City Council's Historians in Residence have worked in neighbourhoods across Dublin City to encourage local people to engage with history, and to promote its sources and discussion, especially the historical collections in Dublin City Library and Archive.

The historians work in the five administrative areas of Dublin City Council to make history and historical sources accessible and enjoyable for all.

In 2020, the Creative Residency @ Richmond Barracks, made by Dublin City Council Culture Company, appointed Dublin's first Historian in Residence for Children. The project seeks to provide space, opportunity and resources to help children uncover the stories of our city and its people. The Historians in Residence are:

- James Curry – Dublin North West Area

- Cormac Moore – Dublin North Central Area

- Mary Muldowney – Dublin Central Area

- Catherine Scuffil – Dublin South City Areas

- Dervilia Roche – Historian in Residence for Children

Dublin City Council's Historian in Residence programme is created by Dublin City Libraries, and is delivered in partnership with Dublin City Council Culture Company.

The Historian in Residence for Children Creative Residency @ Richmond Barracks is a partnership between Dublin City Council Culture Company and Dublin City Libraries.